Algo Trading

Trade Smart and Efficiently Using the Algorithmic Trading System

© Copyright 2024 -Creek Ridge Publishing All rights reserved.

The content contained within this book may not be reproduced, duplicated, or transmitted without direct written permission from the author or the publisher.

Under no circumstances will any blame or legal responsibility be held against the publisher or author for any damages, reparation, or monetary loss due to the information contained within this book, either directly or indirectly.

Legal Notice:

This book is copyright-protected. It is only for personal use. You cannot amend, distribute, sell, use, quote, or paraphrase any part of the content within this book without the consent of the author or publisher.

Disclaimer Notice:

Please note the information contained within this document is for educational and entertainment purposes only. All effort has been executed to present accurate, up-to-date, reliable, and complete information. No warranties of any kind are declared or implied. Readers acknowledge that the author is not engaging in the rendering of legal, financial, medical, or professional advice. The content within this book has been derived from various sources. Please consult a licensed professional before attempting any techniques outlined in this book.

By reading this document, the reader agrees that under no circumstances is the author responsible for any losses, direct or indirect, that are incurred as a result of the use of the information contained within this document, including, but not limited to, errors, omissions, or inaccuracies.

Preface

Become part of the elite group of winning traders by leveraging the power of algorithms!

Are you ready to step up your trading to the next level? Make real money from the markets and **take on every trading setup without losing sleep or money!**

In the trading industry, there's the 90-90-90 rule: "90% of traders lose 90% of their money in the first 90 days." This isn't just a catchy statement. It's the sad reality of the trading industry.

Sooner or later, the majority of aspiring traders find themselves against the rocks of their broken dreams. Don't be part of the losing 90%. You can do that with the help of this trading guide.

Imagine looking at your trading records and seeing a steady climb in profits. Feel what it would be like to go to bed each night and wake up knowing that there's an algorithm generating money on your behalf.

Table of Contents

Introduction

What if there was a way to consistently pull your fair share of the trillions and trillions of dollars that flow through all the financial markets daily without having to lift a finger? It may sound like wishful thinking, but it isn't. Thousands of traders take advantage of the power of algorithms to take advantage of their preferred assets for impressive amounts of money, and you, too, can be one of them.

Gone are the days when you'd have to sit hunched over at your desk, staring at your screen and paying attention to every tick on the charts. Gone are the times when you'd have to wait for hours on end because you're terrified of missing out on a potentially profitable setup. You decided to take up trading for one reason. It's not the money. It's the freedom that the money affords you. So it doesn't make sense for you to trade in one pair of golden handcuffs (your regular, grueling desk job) for another—not when you could have an algorithm do all the hard work on your behalf.

In this short yet informative guide, you'll learn everything you need to get started with algorithmic trading. Unlike every other book out there on this topic, this one is written in simple, easy-to-understand English. You'll find in-depth knowledge and valuable tips and techniques that will help you develop mastery in your trading career.

Are you ready to discover levels of trading success beyond anything you've ever imagined or experienced? Will you seize this one-of-a-kind opportunity to free yourself from the hamster wheel of the nine-to-five life? All you have to do is start with the first chapter. Money may not grow on trees, but as you're about to discover, it's easier to grow with the help of a solid algo.

Chapter 1:

All About Algos

If you're reading this book, you're no stranger to trading, and you've likely heard the term "algo trading" or "algorithmic trading" more often than you care to count. Your curiosity has finally gotten the better of you, and you've decided to look into this algo business and see what it is. What is it about? Why should you bother learning about algos? What possible benefit could this style of trading offer you, and why should you make it part of your trading arsenal? This chapter will give you the answers to all those questions and more.

Algo Trading Defined

Algo trading, also called algorithmic trading, involves using computer programs to execute your trading strategy in the financial markets. Sometimes these programs are also called "expert advisors," a term you're likely familiar with if you work with the popular Metatrader trading platform.

Whether you call them robots, bots, programs, algos, or algorithms, they're designed to scan the markets for specific preset conditions that *you* determine and to execute trades on financial securities when all relevant criteria are met. What makes algorithmic trading different from discretionary trading? Everything is automated. Just click start, and the algo will do the rest of the work for you.

As a discretionary or manual trader, you look at your charts daily to scan for the perfect trading opportunities, looking for technical and fundamental reasons to buy or sell an asset. After hours of sitting at your desk, scanning asset after asset manually, there's more work to be done.

You have to double-check that the asset's price and fundamentals meet your criteria for a good trade according to your strategy's rules before you finally pull the trigger and get into the trade.

You're the one who calculates the perfect position size to put on the line per trade. You decide how long to remain in the trade for whether or not to cut your losses, trail your stop loss, add to your positions, or book partial profits. All of this requires discipline, patience, and focus. It's enough to make you wonder if you have an attention disorder because there's so much information to track, and your conscious mind can barely keep up with it all.

On the flip side, when trading with an algorithm, all of this trouble is taken care of for you by the robot. You preprogram your trusty, efficient worker-bee bot to help you take trades that match the conditions you've instructed it to scan for—and then you take your hands off your mouse and keyboard and let it do all the work for you. That sounds like a dream, doesn't it? Still not convinced you should begin using algorithms to help you with your trading? You'll change your mind soon enough.

The Benefits of Algo Trading

There are multiple reasons the big trading firms employ algorithmic trading as part of their tools to make money from the financial markets. There's no reason good enough for you not to get in on the algo action yourself. Here are several reasons algo trading will revolutionize your trading results.

You couldn't possibly trade as efficiently as an algo. This statement isn't meant to make you feel like a subpar trader or denigrate your results if you've been doing well. It's just the truth.

Can you execute trades in a matter of milliseconds? Can you react quickly to whiplash levels of volatility across all market conditions, such as during news and economic events? Can you click on your platform's buy or sell button in a fraction of a second? Can you generate a slew of orders at the same price in one go? If you can do all these things, then you have no business reading this book.

The speed and efficiency of algo trading means that you can take advantage of the inefficiencies that occur in an asset's price. These inefficiencies do not remain for too long and only a bot could spot them and act fast enough to make them count.

There's a reason high-frequency trading is a thing. Algorithms are programmed to take advantage of every minuscule difference in price that would net you win after win. This technological marvel might as well be magic.

Thanks to the sheer volume of trades trading bots execute in less than a second, you can make yourself a tidy profit. If trading pits were still the order of the day, no one would believe this was possible.

Algo trading takes fear and greed out of the equation. The problem with being human is that you're emotional. This is a good thing when it comes to socializing and interacting with others, but not so much when it comes to your trading. Fear and greed are two of the most prevalent emotions that cause traders to make terrible mistakes that are detrimental to their success.

How often have you let a trade run longer than your strategy's rules say you should, only to have the price turn around and take back the money you left on the table? How often have you hesitated to get into a trade that meets all your criteria because you've been burned by a few losses, only to watch the price move in the direction you anticipated without taking you along for the ride?

If you've always struggled with greed and fear, you should consider trading with algos because they force discipline. A robot doesn't have feelings to keep it from deciding to take a trade. It will take advantage of every opportunity that presents itself according to the parameters you have outlined for it.

It will also get out of a profitable trade while the getting's good, rather than hold on and hope it can make you more money than you programmed it to fetch you. If you consider yourself a phenomenal market analyst but struggle to translate that head knowledge into actual dollars, consider delegating your trades to a robot to do the hard work for you.

Trading algorithms can scan multiple markets at the same time, *all the time.* If you try to do this, you'll burn out. There's no way you can keep your eyes glued to your screen 24/7 and make solid trading decisions. Fortunately, your trading algo doesn't need sleep. All it needs is steady Internet access, and it can take advantage of the opportunities that present itself at any time, no matter the trading session.

If the markets you love to trade are open 24/7, think of the implications of having a robot do the work for you around the clock. It's like having a digital mint that prints money for you day in and day out with no complaints. The best part? You don't have to pay your trading bot commissions or fees to work, and it'll never whine about how you never let it get a moment's rest.

Algorithmic trading saves you money. Since trading bots execute trades much faster than humans can, they can take advantage of quick market movements. They'll handle slippage far better than you could if you traded manually. Slippage is nasty business sometimes. It's what happens when your order is executed at a price far above or below your strike price. It can be positive, but when it's negative, it can cost you.

Your trading robot takes the pain out of risk management. Not only are you less likely to make terrible decisions influenced by fear or greed if you use a robot, but also your algo can help you automatically calculate your position size. How many times have you found the perfect trading opportunity, only to have missed it by a few pips because you were busy calculating your position size or risk for the trade? This is something you won't have to suffer with a trading algorithm.

You can set up a bot so that it follows strict money management rules that cover everything from risk calculation per trade and scaling in and out to stop loss placement, trailing stops, and trade exits. You can even program the algo to stop trading and close all open positions when certain thresholds have been met, for better or worse. With an algo, you can keep your money safe and ensure you have enough chips to play the next opportunity that comes your way.

Drawbacks of Trading with Bots

Now that you know some of the benefits algo trading offers you, how about the drawbacks? It would be remiss not to mention these.

You'll need programming skills to create a bot. If you've never written a line of code a day in your life, this is a problem. Not only do you have to create the bot, but you may need to make changes to it over time too. This may feel like an entry barrier to algo trading but don't despair. You can leave the heavy lifting of coding a bot to expert programmers who understand the financial markets, the dynamics of price action, and the unintelligible lines of code that will bring your robot to life.

Occasionally, the lack of discretion in algo trading may cause losses. As emotional and irrational as humans are, sometimes there's something to be said for the human trait of intuition. Maybe you've experienced this scenario: You're studying the price chart of an underlying asset, and it appears to have provided the perfect opportunity for a great, long trade that will yield you massive profits. It's a textbook trade.

Yet, for some inexplicable reason, you decide to give that setup a miss. You sit it out. Sure enough, moments later, the market plunges to reach new lows. Had you been in that trade that would have been quite a hit to your account.

Unfortunately, you can't program intuition into an algo. Anyone who figures out how to give trading robots a sixth sense will definitely make a killing and perhaps disrupt the economic landscape of the world. For this reason, it's best to check in on what your algorithms are up to now and then rather than leave them to do what you've programmed them to do.

There have been several black swan events, such as the COVID crisis and the Silver Crash, which your algorithm may not have been able to handle, not because you have a terrible strategy but simply because these black swan events are unexpected and incredibly severe. It's wise to intervene with your algo and make adjustments as necessary so you don't go home with a sad story about how you've lost everything but the shirt on your back.

There's always the risk of over-optimizing your trading program. You'll learn how to avoid this mistake later on. Rookie algo traders backtest to curve-fit the results to the market conditions of historical data. The problem with attempting to get phenomenal results across different market conditions from tests is it will inevitably be your downfall.

It's possible to have an algorithm perform astoundingly well with past historical data only to put it to work in live market conditions and have horrific results. The last thing you need is to be fooled by a false sense of security only to go live and have your algorithm make you question your abilities.

These are the drawbacks you have to contend with if you choose to trade with algos. Still, you have to admit that the trade-off is worth it. Besides, if you're not entirely comfortable with the idea of delegating all your trading duties to a robot, you could always blend algo trading with discretionary, manual trading.

Now that you know what algorithmic trading is all about, how it can help you, and what to beware of as you implement it, it's time to talk about how to test the perfect strategy before you code it into a bot.

Chapter 2:

Testing… Is This Thing On?

Pretend you have a child who just turned 16. They've never driven a car a day in their life. For their 15th birthday, you decide you're going to get them a Formula One race car—you know, those cars that reach ridiculous breakneck speeds? You'd never do that. You know your child has to learn the basics of driving before you entrust them with the huge responsibility of such a powerful and possibly dangerous machine.

Similarly, you would never take a strategy you found on some random forum on the Internet or dreamed up while brushing your teeth and put it to the test with live funds. At least, hopefully, you don't do this. Otherwise, you'll burn holes in your pockets—black holes that suck every penny out of your bank account and into oblivion. In this chapter, you'll learn how to properly test your strategy to ensure that it's going to work when you take it out for a drive on the "highway" of the financial markets.

Why should you bother testing your strategies and algos first? If you don't know how to program a bot, you may choose to buy one from a vendor instead. Usually, these robots are advertised with performance reports that can be misleading. You have to understand that the vendor's goal is to get you to buy their product, so they'll do anything to make you think their system is infallible. This is one of the reasons testing is essential. It's not hard to forge or fudge the results of a trading algo to make it appear to be the best thing since sliced bread.

Even if you're not purchasing bots from vendors and decide to create your own, your tests may deceive you. This happens when you optimize your strategy so that it looks great on paper using old data. The trouble is, when you put it to test in real market conditions, this system could fail woefully.

As an algorithmic trader, understand there's every chance that you could receive misleading results from your testing. This is why you should use the best testing practices to eliminate or at least minimize errors in your results. Now, this isn't to imply that testing your strategy using historical data is accurate, but it's better than nothing.

Back Testing

The most common way to test strategies and algorithms is through back-testing with historical data. It's a convenient way to see if you have a viable strategy, but the problem is that it's so easy to mess up the results. How does it work exactly? All you have to do is input the start date and end date of the price action for the financial asset you're analyzing. You can also specify the parameters you'd like to tweak and then let the back-testing platform work out the profitability of your strategy for you. The problem with this is the results you'll get only look amazing because they work for that specific period of price action. What makes this even more insidious is that your system may work for a short while, giving you a false sense of security and the feeling you've found your "Holy Grail" when you haven't, and your winners are due to nothing more than luck.

As a trader, you must have noticed that there are different kinds of market conditions. If the period you selected to test your algo had trending price action, then it makes sense to expect the best results of that strategy only when the market is trending. Apply the same strategy to consolidating market conditions, and you'll be burned. The same applies to strategies designed to take advantage of sideways movement but used in trending conditions. You'll keep buying ceilings and selling floors.

Out-of-Sample Testing — The Antidote to Over-Optimizing

One of the most common mistakes people make as they back test their strategy is using many parameters. As a result, they over-optimize the strategy and make the results seem flawless. Well, you know what they say about things that look too good. Including too many rules in your strategy just to fit it to historical data is a recipe for disaster. This is one of the reasons that brokers often have this line quoted on their sites: *"Past performance is not necessarily indicative of future results."*

If the market of the assets you trade were to somehow repeat the price action you tested your strategy on, bar-for-bar, in that case, you'd have yourself a winner. But as you know, that's not how price action works. The obvious question is, how do you get around this problem? By using out-of-sample testing.

In other words, instead of testing the entire historical data set available to you, you only test about 80% to 90% of it. Then, once you're done making the tweaks you want to your strategy and you're satisfied, you take this newly optimized system and test it out on the remaining 10% to 20% of the data, which is the "out-of-sample" data set.

The result of your out-of-sample testing will be a truer reflection of the capabilities of your trading algorithm in live conditions. This testing system is wonderful because you are applying your strategy or algorithm to market conditions that it has not experienced before after you're done with your modifications instead of trying to tailor your strategy to an arbitrary set of price action bars. It's the closest thing to live testing you can get.

There's a caveat, though. After optimization, the parameters you set your strategy to are forever. This means you'll eventually run into problems when the market conditions inevitably change. This means you'll need a different algo altogether. Otherwise, you'll give back your profits to the market. So, how do you handle this fresh conundrum?

Walk-Forward Testing

The walk-forward test is your solution. Dishonest vendors and lazy, wannabe algorithmic traders won't want to go through the trouble of running a walk-forward test, but you're nothing like them. Roll up your sleeves and get to work, and you'll find the results are worth the time and effort. What does this kind of testing involve? You'll be working with two different data sets to get both optimized results and performance results.

To do this, split your data into two groups—the in-sample set to create your strategy and the out-of-sample set to test said strategy. The point of the first data set is to optimize parameters to your heart's content. At this point of your test, it's okay for you to tweak things until they work for that specific trading period. When done, test the strategy on the out-of-sample data set.

What makes this different from the previous form of testing? You repeat the process multiple times to get a series of out-of-sample results and put them together to give you a more accurate picture of the performance of your strategy.

Ideally, your out-of-sample data sets should have various market conditions for an accurate picture of what your algo could do if you gave it some money and let it play with the markets unsupervised. Whether using it live means you'll become a millionaire or find yourself in debt, the walk-forward test will let you know.

Walk-forward testing is effective—but only when you have all the data you need. What do you do when you're brimming with ideas for a new strategy but don't have enough history to work with? There's only one solution to this problem.

Real-Time Testing

When you're sorely lacking data, use real-time testing. Some of the pros out there don't even bother with any other form of testing because they want to see their strategies in live market conditions. These are the traders who can afford to put real money on the line and see what happens. Why would you want to do this? Because there is no way that you could over-optimize your strategy so it fits old data. You're flying blind here, meaning there's nothing to force your strategy onto, and that's a good thing.

Many traders balk at the thought of real-time testing because there's no way to fast-forward time. It's a slow process that requires loads of patience. If you're a swing or position trader, you may need years before you finally know what the fate of your algo is. This process is made even more tedious because every time you tweak something in your strategy, you have to go back to the beginning. All the results you had before the optimization are no longer valid.

If you're a scalper who trades on short time frames, with each bar lasting minutes or even seconds, you may be able to test your strategy in real-time since you aren't working with higher time frame charts, and you'll have much more data to test with the proper tools. Seconds and minutes pass faster than hours and days, and fortunately, each day has those in spades.

You alone determine the testing methodologies you should use for your strategy. If you intend to make money over the long haul, you should take every word in this chapter to heart. If you don't have the time for real-time testing and don't want to do a walk-forward analysis, your other option is to use back testing and out-of-sample testing, but there's a catch—you can only use your strategy or robot when the market conditions that gave you the best results are replicated on a live chart. That's tricky because no two trading periods are exactly alike.

In other words, if your strategy performs well with consolidations, then only use your programmed algo in periods of consolidation. Once the markets begin to trend, give your algo the day off until things cool down again. The same rule applies if your best test results came from trending markets. Once the slow, sideways chop begins, retire your bot. Now, it's time to talk about the different parts of your strategy.

Chapter 3:

Piecing the Puzzle Together

Most books teach you how to create a strategy before telling you how to test it. This one does things differently on purpose. While anyone can come up with a trading approach, not everyone has the patience to learn how to test it properly, let alone understand why test runs are critical.

Now that you know how to test your strategy to ensure accurate results and are ready to trade live, it's time to discuss developing your trading system. In this chapter, you'll learn valuable information about entries, exits, markets, and time frames, all essential parts of a sound, solid strategy. It will also discuss how to program your trading rules into an algorithm.

Entries, Exits, and Markets

How do you get in? The rules for getting involved in the market are usually the easiest part to figure out. It's unfortunate that too many people are focused on this part alone and do not consider the other aspects that make a trading strategy truly successful. All the gurus and trading groups that advertise high win rates fail to mention the fact that drawdowns are a part of the trading system they're pushing onto you. They're more eager to sell you on the fact that their entries are precise.

If you haven't already, sooner or later, you'll learn that it doesn't matter if you have a crystal ball that correctly predicts the turning points of price. Without the other important aspects of the strategy firmly sorted out, you could still lose and lose big. So don't allow yourself to be seduced by thoughts of the perfect entry. Many novice traders are so enamored with entries because that's the only aspect of the trade they can truly control. Once they put the trade on, they don't know what to do to manage it.

A good rule of thumb is that your entries depend on the sort of trading you do. If you are a position or swing trader, then you don't need to be precise. You can still be profitable even if you get into a trade a little earlier or later than when the entry signal formed.

It's a different story if you're a scalper, though. Since you're only in the markets for a few pips here and there and for minutes or even seconds at a time, every pip matters. Being off by even one pip could severely ruin your profitability.

As for what entry signal you use to get into a trade, that's your call. Some traders use indicators such as moving averages in many ways. For instance, when the price bounces away from a moving average to the downside, they know it's time to go short and vice versa for long trades. Others use trend lines, support and resistance, market structure breaks, etc.

Now, how do you get out? If more traders paid attention to this question, they'd do so much better. To be fair, there is no way to fully control your exits because it's up to the market. The price may push far enough to hit your profit level, or it could stop just short of it and reverse, hitting your stop loss level.

Regardless of what the price does, your exits could make or break your profitability. One of the ways to exit a trade is by looking for the opposite signal of your entry. This is also known as the stop and reverse method and it is excellent if you like to be in the market all the time.

Technical traders love to exit using such tools as candlestick patterns, support, and resistance zones, trend lines, moving averages, etc. Sometimes, they use round figure levels, also called psychological levels, where market participants tend to get in and out of trades. If you choose to go this route, realize that it's possible to have an exit signal trigger right after an entry. To solve this problem, there should be a specific point or zone on the chart beyond which you know your trade idea is invalid. You'll also find it helpful to trade with a specific bias in mind rather than flip-flop between buying and selling.

Some traders simply move their stop losses to break even to cover their commission costs and make their trade risk-free. If the price comes back against them, they won't lose anything. At what point should you move your stop loss? That's entirely up to you and what you've observed about the specific asset you're trading.

Some make their trades risk-free when the market has broken major price structures or swings that were obstacles. Or they'll pick an arbitrary number of pips at which their stops go to break even. If you choose to exit this way, be mindful of the fact that break-even stops cap the money you'd otherwise have made without them if the market price retraces against you, taps your stop loss level, and then resumes moving in your direction.

Some traders love using stop losses, and others hate them. They're there to keep you safe, but at the same time, certain strategies benefit from having a much wider stop or a different way to manage losses. If your stop-loss placement causes you to lose money, then you may need to rethink your entries. When your trade is profitable, you can trail your stop loss to follow the price and allow the market to take you out as it retraces. The downside to trailing stops is you'll cap your upside potential.

If you don't care for using stop losses, you might as well use a take profit order or profit target. There are as many opinions about what makes a proper profit level as there are traders. Sometimes, it helps to allow your profits to run, and other times it doesn't. It all depends on what strategy you're working with. If you take anything away from this portion of the book, let it be this: there's no one-size-fits-all solution to entries and exits. You must use testing to determine what works best for you and your trading style.

What markets will you play in? Some love to trade forex, while others prefer to trade cryptocurrencies. Some prefer indices. Others love to play with stocks. Every market has its unique features that make it different from others. Even within the forex markets, it would be erroneous to assign the same values and strategies to different pairs.

For instance, you may be a scalper who uses a 5-pip stop loss to trade EURUSD with some success. But try to apply that same 5-pip stop loss to a volatile market like GBPNZD, and you'll immediately have your behind handed to you because that is one extremely volatile exotic pair.

How do you figure out which markets should get your hard-earned dollars? You could create a system that works across the board. With this cookie-cutter approach, you will never have to change your strategy regardless of what instrument you're trading.

The good thing about having a strategy that works across all markets is that you can diversify and make even more money. It won't matter if the market conditions continue to change across assets because you have a system that can pull money from every asset class, and there's always at least one with a setup waiting for you to trade it.

Another option is to pick just one asset to trade and create a strategy that specifically works for it. If you enjoy the wild volatility of GBP pairs in forex, then you could create a strategy that works to take advantage of those wild swings. If you prefer majors like EURUSD or AUDUSD because they have smoother, more refined movements and tighter spreads, then your strategy could be tailored to those kinds of pairs.

You could also create a strategy to be traded only in specific market conditions. For instance, if the market is consolidating, a strategy that takes advantage of the fact that price always reverts to the mean would be a good one.

Time Frames

You cannot neglect time frames when creating your strategy. The best time frame to use will depend on the objectives that you have as a trader. If you're a scalper, you may prefer working with the 5-minute time frame and others lower than that (although some say even the 15-minute chart is a scalper's playground). You could also use tick charts if that floats your boat.

If you consider yourself a day trader, use intraday time frames like the 15-minute chart, 30-minute chart, or 1-hour chart to find your setups. Are you a swing trader who holds their trades for a few days at a time? You may prefer working with the 1-hour, 4-hour, and

8-hour charts. Position traders hold their trades for weeks and months on end, so they prefer using daily, weekly, and monthly charts to enter and exit their trades.

If you're a scalper, here's a special note for you. While your playground is on the lower timeframes, you'll find that your trades are more accurate if you analyze higher time frames as well. What looks like a continuation on the lower time frame may be a reversal being set up on a higher time frame. Why does this matter? The higher time frames dictate where the price will go. This will help you with accuracy and precision, as well as positioning yourself to benefit from opportunities. This doesn't suggest you should change your trading style if it works for you. It just means you should keep the big picture in mind.

Do you know that the market is fractal? Take away the time frame label from different charts, and you would not be able to tell the difference—unless, of course, you're dealing with the charts where each bar is only seconds long or tick charts in low-volatility market conditions (those charts look questionable with some assets).

Time and price are fractal no matter what market you're trading. The implication of this is if a strategy works on a lower time frame, it can work on a higher time frame as well, and vice versa. You should still take this with a pinch of salt. Certain time frames may work better for your particular strategy and chosen asset. Also, the higher the time frame, the wider your stop losses and targets.

Some traders prefer analyzing only one time frame, while others use a multi-time frame approach. Making trading decisions based on a single time frame means you aren't distracted or confused about what the price is up to on others. On the other hand, using multiple time frames means you'll have more context for possible price action in the future, and you may find that you're coming up against support or resistance or that you could have a higher profit level than a single time frame would suggest.

The traders who work with multiple charts usually have at least three time frames. The highest one gives them the lay of the land and gives them directional bias. The second time frame is lower or faster than the highest, and it's where traders get a signal that their setup is forming. The final time frame is even faster or lower than the second, which means traders can refine their entries to achieve tighter stop losses and maximize the profit potential of the trade.

Programming Your Strategy

You have all the puzzle pieces to create your perfect strategy. You've tested it. It works pretty well. The question is, how do you program the strategy? After all, you didn't pick up this book to learn about discretionary trading. You want to learn how to make algos do the bulk of the work and give you an easier life.

If programming isn't your forte, you could learn how to code these expert advisors or algorithms yourself with your preferred trading platform. If you're uninterested in learning to program expert advisors, you don't have to. There are online marketplaces like MQL5 where you can get an expert to code your algorithm according to the specifications of your strategy. You could even hire someone off of Fiverr or Upwork.

The downside to outsourcing your programming needs is that you may have to make a few tweaks to your expert advisor or algo. It's going to cost you every time.

What if you don't have money to spend on hiring an expert programmer? You don't have to spend a dime if you don't want to. If you're certain your strategy is solid, team up with someone who has programming knowledge. You let them know your strategy, they automate it, and you both enjoy using this robot to make cool cash.

The only challenge you may face is finding someone you can trust who won't just run off with your strategy and leave you high and dry with no robot.

If you can find the time, learn how to program. There are so many resources available on the Internet you can use to teach yourself to code algorithms. Many of these resources are free, but if you prefer to be under the guidance of skilled hands, then you could always pay for an online class.

The great thing about learning this new skill is no one can take it away from you. You can monetize it, and not only that, but you will enjoy knowing you can accurately test any new strategy you come up with in the future and create the bot so it works exactly as you need it to. So pay for a coding class or invest time in studying free coding material, and your efforts will be rewarded richly.

So, you know how to build a strategy from scratch. You realize that every element of the strategy matters as much as the others. You also know what to do to turn this winning strategy of yours into an algorithm. There's one thing that could get in the way of your progress if you don't look into it. Find out what that is in the next chapter.

Chapter 4:

Money, Money, Money

You could have the most profitable strategy in the trading world and yet still be a loser. How is that possible? Many traders who experience this baffling conundrum are terrible at managing money. Losing streaks happen even to the best of traders.

Once novices discover they have a powerful system on their hands, all they can think of is how they want to start making thousands of dollars per second right this red hot minute. They get greedy and put on position sizes too large for their account balances to handle. Some get lucky in the beginning and don't realize this is a bad habit they must nip in the bud. Eventually, they crash and burn.

Some have figured out their position sizes and strategy but still can't turn things around to make profits from the markets. With these traders, the odds are they haven't understood the power of a good risk-to-reward ratio and don't know what the win rate of their strategy is.

This chapter will teach you everything you need to know about handling your money like a pro and handling the losing streaks when they come. There's no sugarcoating it: Losses *will* come. It is a statistical fact that you will encounter a string of losers at some point, no matter how accurate your system is.

Position Sizes

Every trader had dreams of being able to capture ridiculous amounts of profits that would "10X" their original balance. The only traders who still dream of this fantasy are novices. The truth about trades like these as they are rare. If you hold out for them, refusing to take profits when you should because you think a trade has more to give, you'll lose.

Eventually, you may not have enough capital to take advantage of the opportunities as they arise—and how uncanny is it that those massive moves come just as your broker sends you a margin call and you only have a few cents left in your account?

The same fate awaits you if you put a big chunk of your capital on the line enough for just one trade because you "feel" it's going to be a home run. That's why you need to learn proper position sizing techniques.

Your position is how much money you put up for a trade. It could be a short position, which means selling, or a long one, which means buying. When you aren't in the market at all, you're flat or square.

Position sizing is about choosing the proper trade size to sell or buy the underlying asset you're trading. You should always know how much you're going to risk before you put a trade on. Not only that but also how badly your account balance will be hit if that trade turns out to be a loser.

Those who are new to trading take a gut-feeling approach to managing their position sizes. Of course, that never ends well for them. You need to have a proper risk management plan in place. It's a key part of your strategy. If one loss is enough to give your account a significant dent, then there's something wrong.

The best way to mitigate losses from terrible position sizing is to think of your algorithm not just as a money-making tool but as a risk management tool as well. More than that, you should prioritize risk management as you program this robot.

Using proper position sizing will keep you from losing excessively and help you make the best of your winners. If your position sizes are so small as to be insignificant, you have to make peace with the fact that you are never going to make a livable income from trading. It's all about balance. So, what are the best position sizing techniques you could use to keep your risk in check while enjoying your rewards?

You could use a fixed dollar value. If you're new to trading, you'll appreciate the simplicity of this particular position size management technique. It's also a great one for the times when you don't have a lot of capital. How does it work? All you have to do is assign a fixed dollar amount to each trade. Remember to account for trading fees like commissions and swaps.

Here's how the fixed dollar value position size technique works. Assume that you have $100,000. You may decide that you would like to risk $10,000 for each trade. If you do, you have 10 shots to get it right before you go bust. You probably even have fewer tries than 10 since there will be trading fees, slippage, and other costs.

A better option could be to risk only $1,000 for each trade, which means you have a little under 100 tries to get a winning trade—and if your strategy or algorithm is so terrible that you're losing up to 80 trades in a row, then you have to go back to the drawing board.

You could risk a fixed percentage. This is another popular position sizing technique. Decide before you come to the charts what percentage of your account balance you want to put on the line per trade. This method is an industry-standard practice, popular in forex and other financial markets.

A good rule of thumb is to risk no more than 1% to 2% of your overall capital per trade. Back to the analogy of your fictional $100,000 account balance. Risking 1% to 2% of that means each of your trades should only cost you $1,000 to $2,000 each.

You may fall in love with this particular position sizing strategy because you aren't capping your profit potential. If you use the fixed dollar method, your account balance will grow, but the profits won't match the size of your capital, as you'll be leaving money on the table. Your equity curve isn't as impressive with that position sizing technique as it is when you use a fixed percentage risk.

For instance, if you grow your $100,000 account to $200,000 with the former technique, you'd still be risking $1,000 per trade. Assuming you are rewarded three times more than what you put on the line, you'll still earn $3,000. However, with the fixed percentage risk, you will be risking $2,000 per trade, which will bring you $6,000 for every winning trade.

The trader who pays attention to percentages instead of dollar signs will last long and enjoy a profitable career. Every time your account balance increases, you're still keeping your risk at 1%, but you enjoy more profits than before. Even when you lose, you know you only put 1% on the line. That's why this is known as an anti-martingale strategy. There's no reason to up or drop your risk with each loss or win.

Be mindful of how much money you are putting on the line and if you can afford to lose that amount. Do you find you can't sleep at night because of a running trade? Then, your position size is too large. Cut your losses by closing it, and if you're in profit, don't get greedy by letting it run without reducing the size. If you do, you'll teach yourself that risky behavior is worth the payoff, and one day, it *won't* be.

You'll also know you've bitten off more than you can chew when you feel discomfort after putting on the trade. When this happens, do not hope or pray because that is a great way to lose money. Accept that you've made a mistake and close the position immediately, or reduce your risk by closing it partially.

There's no reason to allow a large loss to become even larger because you hope the market will turn around and have mercy on you. Natural losing streaks are one thing, but it's another thing entirely when you're suffering a losing streak because of greed. That's why thinking in percentages is much better. 1% could be $1 or $10,000, but it's still plain, boring 1%. When it comes to trading, boring is good. Boring should become your best friend.

Risk to Reward Ratio vs. Win Rate

Some argue that a healthy risk-to-reward ratio is better than a high win rate. This is an age-old debate that traders still engage in today. The truth is, both of these things matter, and you have to find the balance between them.

The risk-to-reward ratio refers to how much money you put on the line (your risk) versus how much you get back per trade (your reward). If you make three for every dollar you risk, then your risk-to-reward ratio is 1:3. What about your win rate? It's how often you win. Usually, the win rate is written as a percentage. If you win 70 out of every 100 trades, you have a win rate of 70%.

When you have a strategy with a high win rate, the trade-off is that its risk-to-reward ratio is usually rather low. On the flip side, if you have a high risk-to-reward ratio, chances are your win rate is low. There's a reason many traders focus more on their win rates than their risk-to-reward ratio. They hate it when they are wrong. Unfortunately, there is no way to be in the trading industry without losing trades here and there. It's par for the course. Call it the cost of doing business, if you will. But here's the thing: Having losing trades doesn't equal a losing algorithm or strategy. You'll come to understand this shortly.

Assume, for a moment, that every time you put a trade on, you're putting $100 on the line. You've created a system that guarantees you at least 7 times your risk as a reward. Not wanting to be greedy, you've decided to exit your trades once you're up by 5 times your risk. The wonderful thing about this risk-to-reward ratio of yours is even if you lose 80% of your trades (as in, you have a win rate of 20%), you'll still come out on top.

If you lose 8 trades, you're set back by $800. However, you have two winning trades which total $1,000 in your favor. Overall, you're up by $200. That's the power of a good risk-to-reward ratio.

It's a good rule of thumb to at least have a risk-to-reward ratio of 1:2. In other words, you should get back at least twice what you put in per trade. Note that if you gun for a higher ratio than that, you'll likely have more losses, but at least your wins will cover the costs of your losses, and you'll have spare change. This is the reason you can't conclude a few losing trades means your strategy should be decapitated by the Red Queen. Also, when you hit a winning streak (yes, those happen, too), your healthy risk-to-reward ratio will compound your account balance dramatically.

Now, imagine you put $500 on the line for each of your trades, but you win only $100 each time. Say you have a win rate of 90%, which means that out of every 10 trades, 9 of them are blue. Your winners would total $900, while that one loss would be a whopping $500. Your total profit is $400.

You may take this as a win, but consider this: What happens when you lose 2, 3, or even 4 trades in a row? It should immediately become apparent to you how this inverse risk-to-reward ratio with the high win rate could be a sure way of losing money.

Some traders don't mind sacrificing the concept of a good risk-to-reward ratio on the altar of high win rates. The way they see it, they allocate specific dollar amounts to their trading balances each time they trade.

If they make money, they're fine with it. If that account blows up in their favorites, they can simply reload and have another go at the markets.

Here's a scenario to help you understand that thought process. Imagine you have $10,000 to trade with. You want to try this high-win rate, low-risk-to-reward technique. So, you fund your account with only $1,000. You plan to risk $50 for a reward of $25 per trade.

If the worst happens and you lose all the money in your account, you still have $9,000 to play with. So, add another $1,000 and try again. Nothing's stopping you from taking this route to trading success, as crazy as it sounds. Maybe you can make it work, but here's some advice that will save you pain in the future: at least develop a few strategies that have a good risk-to-reward ratio. Split your trading capital, using some money for your conservative strategy with your reasonable risk-to-reward, and the rest of it for your aggressive, high-win rate system. This way, your trading portfolio is balanced, and you're less likely to take a critical blow that causes you to call it quits with trading.

Whatever you decide, remember you can either have a good risk-to-reward ratio or a high win rate.

You don't get both. That's a mathematical fact, not an attempt at being a "vibe killer."

Dealing with Losing Streaks

As the living trading legend Tom Hougaard put it, "The best loser wins." The man must know what he's talking about since he wrote a whole book with that same title. If you're going to win at trading the financial markets, you have to win at losing, too.

It is simply impossible to avoid losing streaks in your trading career, regardless of how much success you've had or how many years of experience are under your belt. Instead of hoping and praying that losing streaks never come your way, preparing to handle them like a pro is better.

When people take up trading as a profession, all they see are dollar signs. They don't realize that risk management is a huge part of their job as professional traders. Perhaps someone should force all traders to identify as risk managers and abolish other professional titles. That might do a good thing or two for everyone's trading psychology.

How do you lose like a winner? It all begins with acceptance. Accept that losing trades are part of the game.

Make peace with the fact that you will have losing days. Measure your trading performance not in terms of days and weeks but in months, even quarters. Look at your trades not only individually, but as an aggregate over time.

Before you run your algorithm, contemplate the fact that the next trade it takes, which is the picture-perfect setup, could turn out to be a loser. That should help you adjust your position size properly if you haven't done so already. Realize that you're playing the long game. That's where you'll find success, not in the short bursts of booms and busts that a losing trader's equity and drawdown curves tell horror stories about.

If you think about it, there's really no difference between a psychic with a crystal ball and a trader analyzing their charts. Sure, you could tell yourself that you're using statistical edges and you've tested everything under the sun and you have the perfect system. However, if there is one similarity between the trading business and psychic readings, it's that there is always an element of uncertainty.

The psychic reading could be wrong because the client in question made different life choices that changed their life's trajectory, or the "psychic" was a quack to begin with. Similarly, a trader could be wrong about their "A+++" setup because they missed something or the market simply did not want to respond as they expected it to. Professional traders know that every time they put on a trade, they might as well kiss the money they risked goodbye. That's the attitude you should have as your algo places each trade.

If you can't let go of the money you assign to a trade, remember to pause your algo and set a more appropriate position size. You know, a size that doesn't make your belly ache or give you sweaty pits in the middle of a snowy winter. You'll make money from algo trading with a solid strategy if you let time do its thing rather than force your riches to come this second only to lose what little you have.

Once more, how do you lose like a winner? The following tips will prove useful.

Set a fixed loss percentage for each day or week. Once that threshold has been hit, shut down your algorithm, close your trading platform, and walk away from your computer. You'd better not have the mobile version of your trading platform on your phone, either, so you don't act impulsively and make a bad situation worse. Your mind can only handle so many hits before you begin making emotional, irrational, and detrimental decisions. This happens even to the best of traders.

Thankfully, you're trading with an algorithm, which means you can program it to stop taking trades once the loss limit for the day or week has been hit. Sure, you could tweak it to keep going, but that would require extra steps. Hopefully, the time you spend clicking around to restart your bot should be enough for you to recognize it's best to let this losing day go and try again next time. Revenge trading is never worth it, you know.

Review your losing trades. Don't do this right after you lose because you may be too emotional to see what went wrong. Instead, give it a day or so. The reason it's essential to review losers is that you need to know if you have a problem with your system or if your algorithm is not following the rules you've programmed it to.

If your system is just fine and the algorithm is working as it should, then the odds are it was simply one of the regular losers that happen now and then. Either way, losing trades offer valuable information that you can turn to your advantage. Don't miss out on the powerful lessons they can teach you.

Prioritize your risk-to-reward ratio. Unless your system has been specifically optimized for a high win rate, focus on getting the most bang for your buck. So as you program your algorithm, set it up to ignore any trading opportunity that offers you a reward far less than your risk. This way, you avoid losing in the long run.

Switch to a demo account. If you're still in the honeymoon phase of trading and excited about always being in the market, but you've lost a significant amount, don't worry, it'll pass. In the meantime, switch to a demo account and allow your algorithm to continue trading that instead. Unless you're a financial masochist, there's no reason to put yourself through the endless torture of losing dollar after dollar, watching your balance go from a bunch of zeroes to just one zero.

Take time off from the markets. There's no reason to get upset with yourself or your algorithm when you hit a losing streak. It could be that the present trading conditions aren't optimal for your strategy.

Remind yourself what you designed your strategy to accomplish and double-check to see if the market conditions are the same as what your bot is trained to handle. When you realize that the market is indeed not in the correct phase for your strategy, close up shop and call it a day. Or at least give it a few hours before you return to see if things are back on track.

You're on your way to becoming a profitable, professional algorithmic trader. There are just a few more things to go over. If you want to equip yourself with the last of the tools you need to succeed as an algo trader, head to the final chapter.

Chapter 5:

All Systems Go

You've decided to take the plunge and trade with algos. You're convinced that algo trading is just what you've been looking for. You love the idea that, finally, you don't have to sit at your charts for hours on end with your eyes glued to your screen and your retinas screaming for mercy. You're ready and raring to go. That's great and all, but hold on a moment. You need the last pieces of the puzzle and then you can be on your merry way.

Demo Dollars vs. Live Dollars

The beautiful thing about monopoly money is, that even if you lose it all, at least you'll still have dinner and a roof over your head. The same thing applies when it comes to trading with a demo account using demo dollars. Your demo account has been given to you for a reason. Some say it's free because the brokers want you to practice terrible trading habits, get used to them, and then take them live so they can take you to the cleaners. How willing are you to bet that those people also probably have an impressive collection of tinfoil hats?

Your demo account is a powerful tool. It's all a matter of perspective. Whether you're testing new strategies or using your demo account to restrain yourself from taking unnecessary live trades, you must admit there's some value to these imaginary dollars on your screen. Also, if you treat your demo account as a live one, it's an excellent playground to give your discipline muscles a good workout and keep your expectations rooted in reality.

There's a caveat. You can only use your algorithm on your demo account for so long. At some point, you realize it's time to stop playing and make some real money. Now, pay attention. One of the most confounding things about demo trading compared to live trading is that there are completely different mindsets at work in each scenario.

Some traders—whether discretionary or algorithmic—do exceptionally well with a demo account and feel they are prepared to make a killing when they go live. They go live, and *the market* does the killing, cleaning out their accounts.

Now, you'd assume that by trading with algorithms, you don't have to worry about being in this situation. The problem is you still need self-control. You see, some traders use their algorithms as designed, following the rules to the letter when it's their demo account. But the minute they switch from demo trading to live trading, something else takes over them. They begin to tweak the settings of their algorithm even though they know they shouldn't.

It's easy to beat your chest with pride and say, "Couldn't be me," but it's happened to most people, even the best of traders. Knowing you're capable of losing control and tweaking settings you shouldn't is the first step to catching yourself when the impulse to change things hits you.

The psychology of live trading versus that of demo trading are two different beasts. So, when you finally decide your algorithm is ready to go live, do yourself a favor and drop your risk even lower than what you used in your demo trading. Keep the risk percentage low for a week or two, and then gradually bring it back up as you lose the excitement of trading in a live environment with your algo.

A note on excitement: This interesting emotion is usually accompanied by optimism. Whether that optimism is warranted or not is another matter.

The problem with excitement is it leads to critical levels of optimism bordering on overconfidence.

You become too easy-going with your position sizes and risk management—much to your detriment. If you're unfortunate enough to win a recklessly sized trade, greed, and pride join the party. You think you can get away with another reckless trade and maybe a couple more. You're in too deep now, too far gone to stop. It's all fun and games until you've lost 60% of your trading balance in one day as a result of these emotions. This is a story thousands of traders can relate to. You don't have to be a statistic.

So, kick off your live algo trading journey by starting with even lower risk percentages than you originally planned. Pick a risk percentage so low and dull that it makes dishwater seem fascinating. You could set your algo to only risk 0.1% per trade.

This way, your focus is on allowing your algorithm to work as you intended it to, checking to ensure it performs well in live conditions, and curbing your excitement into nonexistence so it can't invite its distant destructive cousins (overconfidence, pride, and greed) over to have a party sponsored by your trading balance.

Choosing a Broker

You can't trade without a broker. Every day, a new firm pops up and pushes their no-deposit bonus offer in your face, hoping you'll give them a handsome chunk of change. The question is, how do you choose the best one in the face of so many options?

1. Choose regulated brokers only. This way, if the broker goes bust, your money's safe and recoverable.

2. Confirm that they offer state-of-the-art trading platforms that are fast, easy to use, and able to handle algorithmic and programming functions.

3. You want a broker that offers the tightest spreads available in the industry. This will be a good thing for your account balance in the long run. Wide spreads take much longer to get into profit.

4. Read reviews to ensure the broker you're choosing instantly executes your trades. With algorithms, every second counts—especially if your strategy requires precision. Pick an ECN broker rather than a market maker for instant executions at true prices.

5. Your broker should have multiple avenues to offer you support as you need it. So check what the reviews say about the customer support of a brokerage firm before you settle on it.

6. Your broker should have no problems with processing withdrawals and deposits speedily. There's no reason it should take a whole week to see your funds reflected in your bank account. If that happens, consider getting a different broker.

Funding Your Account

From your testing, it should be obvious how much money you need to put into your account to run your algorithm. If you put in too little capital at the beginning, there's a chance you will run out of money before your system has a chance. Drawdown is a part of the trading process. Note that you may want to add a little something extra to your starting balance to cover the margin costs, too. If you don't add the margin, then you may hit your drawdown limits much earlier than you should since those costs will eat into your balance. So, check with your broker to learn more about the costs.

You shouldn't put in too much capital, either. There's no reason to risk more than necessary and cause yourself financial heartbreak. Remember the importance of setting a loss limit. That practice should still apply even in live trading.

Trading with Backup

Trading is a lonely profession, but the kind of backup being referred to in this section has nothing to do with finding someone to be the trading Robin to your Batman.

There are other risks to address in trading besides losing your account due to terrible strategies with deceitful or misleading performance results or a badly programmed algo. It's a jungle out on these trading streets. Anything could get you at any point, and that's why you need to be prepared.

Your computer could crash on you. Your Internet Service Provider could suddenly experience downtime. Your broker may have a problem with their price feed delivery. How do you handle these issues?

You need backup. Ideally, you should have more than one computer, just in case your usual one acts up or crashes. To store testing and other data, get backup storage. Don't settle for storing all of your information online in the cloud either. Back up what you have online offline on good old-fashioned physical hard drives.

Power outages are rare, but what if the power's cut in the middle of one of the most important trades of your life? What if you didn't get the chance to place your stop loss, and the worst occurs while the power is out? To avoid this, get yourself a backup power supply.

Don't kid yourself by assuming you could never lose power because it hasn't happened in your neck of the woods in decades. There's a first time for everything. It also helps to have an extra phone line so that you can reach your broker in case there's something wrong with your primary line.

Speaking of brokers, it doesn't hurt to have more than a few in your back pocket. It's not unheard of for a too-big-to-fail broker to suddenly pack up and quit their business or struggle with other issues that affect you and your trades. You don't want their decisions to impact you negatively or get between you and your algo profits. So, register with more than one reliable, regulated broker.

Using a VPS

The acronym VPS is short for Virtual Private Server. If you ever experience downtime during your trading or you notice a lag in the data being delivered to your screen because your Internet is acting up, it's great to have a VPS. With this server, it doesn't matter if your computer is on or off. You install your trading platform on a virtual machine or computer, which stays online unless there's a scheduled maintenance or something—and typically, the VPS provider will give you a heads up if they're about to go down so you can prepare for that accordingly.

Trading with a VPS sets your mind at ease. It means never having to miss out on profits or trades. If your algorithm's strategy is designed to work around the clock regardless of the trading session, it makes sense to have it running on your VPS to keep making money.

Is your algorithm based on a scalping strategy? That's even more reason for you to invest in getting a VPS. You'll never have to worry about lags that cause you to lose precious money or slip you into trades at the worst possible prices. It's worth the monthly fee once you have an algo that works well enough to let you withdraw a sizeable amount of money whenever you wish.

Conclusion

You now have everything you need to start algo trading, but this doesn't mean you have nothing more to learn on the subject. Think of this book as a starting guide, a powerful kit to set you on your path to success and greatness by leveraging the power of robots in your trading career.

In a world where artificial intelligence is increasingly taking over many sectors of the economy, it only makes sense for you to keep a finger on the pulse of the trading industry and track the innovations that will revolutionize algorithmic trading as you know it. If you want to be ahead of the losing 90%, you'll need to keep your ears to the ground.

As you transition from manual or discretionary trading to algorithmic trading, maintain a positive attitude, and you'll find the storms easier to bear. Challenges are inevitable, but if you remain resilient, you'll overcome them. It's only a matter of time before you wonder why you never looked into algo trading before now. When that happens, you'll never look back, and there'll be no stopping your greatness.

For now, don't allow yourself to be frustrated by the hiccups you experience as you work on your algorithms and strategies. Learn from every failed experiment, and you'll achieve better results with each new iteration of your algo.

While you're at it, don't get suckered in by those who claim they have the "Holy Grail" of expert advisors or algos. The trading industry has its fair share of snake oil salesmen. They've been there since its inception, and they're not going anywhere anytime soon.

So, the onus is on you to be vigilant about what you're being sold and do your homework before you go live with any vendor's product. If anyone promises you a strategy that's "completely risk-free" and has a "99% win rate," you should run for the hills—or in whatever direction will get you as far away from them as possible.

Getting started with algorithms will take a fair bit of work, but eventually, it will pay off. Plan to accomplish your algo trading goals and then follow it, making adjustments as needed. Test every strategy extensively before you program it into an algorithmic system. Then, test your algo rigorously before you deploy it in a live market.

Finally, whenever you get the chance, work with other traders who are just as passionate about trading with algos as you are. You know how the saying goes. "Two heads are better than one." By teaming up with other traders and programmers, you could brainstorm some of the most fantastic ideas, automate them, and make a killing in any market. You'll get where you want to go further and faster when you work with a team of algo trading enthusiasts.

What are you waiting for? Get to it already. Success is just around the corner.

References

Bao, T., Nekrasova, E., Neugebauer, T., & Riyanto, Y. E. (2021). Algorithmic Trading in Experimental Markets with Human Traders: A Literature Survey. *SSRN Electronic Journal.* https://doi.org/10.2139/ssrn.3908065

Boehmer, E., Fong, K. Y. L., & Wu, J. (Julie). (2015). International Evidence on Algorithmic Trading. *SSRN Electronic Journal.* https://doi.org/10.2139/ssrn.2022034

Burgess, N. (2019). An Introduction to Algorithmic Trading: Opportunities & Challenges within the Systematic Trading Industry. *SSRN Electronic Journal.* Social Science Research Network Electronic Journal. https://doi.org/10.2139/ssrn.3466213

CFI Team. (2015). *Algorithmic Trading.* Corporate Finance Institute. https://corporatefinanceinstitute.com/resources/equities/algorithmic-trading/

Chan, E. P. (2017). *Machine Trading: Deploying Computer Algorithms to Conquer the Markets.* Wiley.

Chan, E. P. (2021). *Quantitative Trading: How to Build Your Own Algorithmic Trading Business.* John Wiley & Sons, Inc.

Donadio, S., & Ghosh, S. (2019). *Learn Algorithmic Trading: Bbuild and Deploy Algorithmic Trading Systems and Strategies using Python and Advanced Data Analysis.* Packt Publishing Ltd.

Donefer, B. S. (2010). Algos Gone Wild: Risk in the World of Automated Trading Strategies. *The Journal of Trading, 5*(2), 31–34. https://doi.org/10.3905/jot.2010.5.2.031

Evans, C., Pappas, K., & Xhafa, F. (2013). Utilizing Artificial Neural Networks and Genetic Algorithms to Build an Algo-Trading Model for Intra-Day Foreign Exchange Speculation. *Mathematical and Computer Modelling, 58*(5-6), 1249–1266. https://doi.org/10.1016/j.mcm.2013.02.002

Fama, E. F., & Blume, M. E. (1966). Filter Rules and Stock-Market Trading. *The Journal of Business, 39*(S1), 226. https://doi.org/10.1086/294849

Kissell, R. (2019). *The Science of Algorithmic Trading and Portfolio Management*. Elsevier Academic Press.

Pruitt, G. (2016). *The Ultimate Algorithmic Trading System Toolbox + Website Using Today's Technology to Help You Become a Better Trader*. Hoboken, New Jersey Wiley.

Saleem Arnuk, & Saluzzi, J. (2012). *Broken Markets: How High Frequency Trading and Predatory Practices on Wall Street Are Destroying Investor Confidence and Your Portfolio*. FT Press.

Seth, S. (2023). *Basics of Algorithmic Trading: Concepts and Examples*. Investopedia. https://www.investopedia.com/articles/active-trading/101014/basics-algorithmic-trading-concepts-and-examples.asp

www.ingramcontent.com/pod-product-compliance
Lightning Source LLC
Chambersburg PA
CBHW050808160726

48004CB00002B/757